Yukon Adventures
MAGAZINE

FOUR INFORMATIONAL TEXTS

by Jeanette Leardi

Table of Contents

Informational Texts

What is an informational text?

Informational text is nonfiction text that presents information in an accurate and organized way. It is often about a single subject such as an event or time period in history or a scientific discovery. It may be about any topic, such as a sport or a hobby. The research report that you write for a school assignment is an informational text. An article you read in your favorite fashion magazine or on a Web site is an informational text, too. A newspaper account of a local election and a history book chapter on a famous battle are additional examples of informational texts.

What is the purpose of informational texts?

Informational text has one main purpose: to inform. The best informational writing does this in a way that keeps readers' attention. It pulls readers in, making them want to keep reading and to know more about the topic.

How do you read an informational text?

When you read informational text, look for facts and for the details that support them. Read critically to make sure conclusions make sense. If there is more than one way to look at an event or situation, make sure it is given. Ask questions: *Did I learn something new from this text? Do I want to know more about it? Can I draw my own conclusions from what I have read?*

Features of an Informational Text

The text has a strong beginning that hooks the reader.

The text has a strong ending that keeps readers thinking.

The information is accurate and the facts have been checked.

The text includes multiple perspectives so that the reader can draw his or her own conclusions.

The text uses primary sources when appropriate.

The text has a logical organization of major concepts.

The information includes graphics that support the text.

Who writes informational texts?

Writers who know their topic well write good informational text. They do this by becoming mini-experts on the subjects they are writing about. They make sure that they support the information in their work with historical facts, scientific data, graphics such as time lines and diagrams, and expert evidence. They provide more than one person's point of view. They use primary sources, firsthand information like journals and photographs.

Tools for Readers and Writers

Graphic and Text Features

Informational text writers often include text and graphic features to support their ideas and help readers understand what they are saying. Graphic features including photographs, maps, charts, lists, illustrations, and diagrams help the reader interpret the texts. By interpreting the text, readers make inferences, draw conclusions, build summaries, and identify what is important. Text features including bullets, sidebar text, colored fonts, and chapter headings help readers locate information because it stands out from the main text.

Superlatives

Superlatives are special adjectives that are used to compare three or more things. Some superlatives end in **-est**, while others are preceded by the word **most**. Superlatives ending in **-est** include **biggest**, **littlest**, and **prettiest**. **Most** superlatives include **most beautiful** and **most organized**.

Identify Main Idea and Supporting Details

When reading nonfiction, look for the author's main ideas about the topic. Search for details that the author uses to support those main ideas. Main ideas often appear in the topic sentence of a paragraph. These main ideas are called stated main ideas. Other times, readers must use what they read to guess or infer the main idea. These main ideas are called unstated, or implied, main ideas. Reducing several pages of text to a couple of main ideas can help the reader understand and remember what has been read.

Welcome to *Yukon Adventures* Magazine

The cold and snowy Yukon is one of Canada's smallest and least-populated territories. It is named for the nearly 2,000-mile (3,218.7-kilometer) long Yukon River that flows from British Columbia, through the Yukon, and into Alaska.

Our magazine celebrates the rich history, culture, and traditions of the area where the mighty Yukon flows. Many different groups of people have lived here over the centuries, including the Inuit. Today, the Inuit population is very small. In this issue you'll read how Inuit elders pass along their stories and traditions to the young. The Gold Rush of the late 1800s took place in the Yukon. Prospectors hoping to strike it rich traveled north in record numbers. Find out what it took to be a prospector and then decide if you would have taken on that challenge.

Or maybe you would prefer the challenge of the world's most famous dog sled race, the Iditarod. The annual, multi-day race spans 1,100 miles (1,770.3 kilometers) of Alaskan wilderness. Ironically, that distance has another meaning for Alaskans. That is how much coastline was affected by the *Exxon Valdez* oil spill of 1989. We'll revisit the area and report on the results of the cleanup.

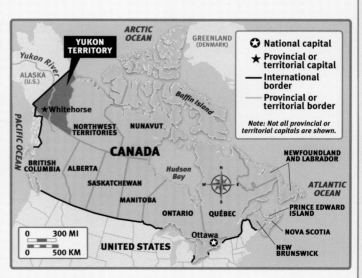

Alaska's Iditarod:

A Grueling Test of Person and Dog

March 6, 2010, 9:59 A.M. Anchorage, Alaska. It's a biting 25° Fahrenheit (−3.9° Celsius), but the windchill makes it feel like 16°F (−8.9°C). A crowd of 30,000 people cheer excitedly. The thirty-eighth Iditarod Trail Sled Dog Race is about to begin!

Seventy-two mushers, or sled drivers, and their teams of dogs are at the starting line. They are ready to compete for more than half a million dollars in prize money. The mushers can barely control either their own excitement or that of their restless, barking dogs. It's as if the teams of twelve to sixteen dogs can sense that they are about to go on the most important run of their lives.

The race will take them to Nome, Alaska, over 1,100 miles

(1,770.3 kilometers) away. It will take at least eight days for the first team to cross the finish line. The route will carry them through some of the **most challenging** wilderness on Earth. Who will make it to the end? More importantly, who will win?

Strength and Skill

From its official beginning in 1973 and for years before, the Iditarod has been an annual contest of strength, skill, and endurance. Only the **most skillful** teams can safely navigate the long and difficult course. Each dog sled has a GPS device that sends out signals if the sled veers off course and gets lost. But mushers can't use a GPS device to guide them. Instead, they must follow the route the old-fashioned way, using only maps and a compass while racing through blizzards, ice, and snowdrifts several feet high.

When it comes to pulling heavy loads over great distances, Alaskan huskies are the right dogs for the job. They can run for hundreds of miles on very little rest. And that's just what they do during the Iditarod. Throughout the entire race, a musher and his or her dogs are allowed only two 8-hour rest stops and one required 24-hour rest stop. The Iditarod is one of the **most grueling** races on Earth.

During odd-numbered years, Iditarod race teams travel the Southern Route on their way from Anchorage to Nome. In even-numbered years, they use the Northern Route.

A Race That Honors Alaska's Past

The Iditarod is one of the few opportunities people have to see a dog sled team in action today. But that wasn't always the case. In fact, a century ago, dog sledding was the main way to get around in Alaska. People used dog sleds to go hunting and to carry back the animals they had killed for food.

In the late nineteenth century, gold was discovered in Alaska and the Klondike Gold Rush began. In 1909, a large amount of gold was discovered in a place called Iditarod. One dog sled path became the main route to the town and was known as the Iditarod Trail. The trail eventually became the main route for bringing settlers, groceries, and mail throughout Alaska. Today, Alaskans use planes, trains, trucks, and snowmobiles to get around.

The Iditarod Trail Sled Dog Race honors Alaska's pioneer past and the crucial role that dog sledding played in its past. In the 1920s, airplanes began to replace dog sleds as the primary means of transportation—but the dogs had one last day of glory. In the winter of 1925, an illness called diphtheria swept through Nome. The people needed a special medicine. But the waters around Nome were frozen and no ships could get through. There were no roads for cars. Bad weather made it impossible for any plane to fly. So the medicine was put on a train in Anchorage and delivered to a town called Nenana. From there, mushers formed relay teams. They traveled nearly 700 miles (1,126.5 kilometers) by dog sled to get the medicine to Nome. The mushers and dogs helped save many lives!

The first dog sled team arrives in Nome with diphtheria medicine, March 18, 1925.

9

March 16, 2:59 p.m. Nome, Alaska. Lance Mackey and his team of eleven dogs cross the finish line! Lance, an Alaskan native, has won his fourth straight Iditarod. No one else in history has ever won four times in a row. Lance comes from a family of Iditarod champions. His father won in 1978. His older brother won in 1983.

2010 Iditarod Results: Top 5 Finishers						
Pos.	Musher	Time In	Dogs In	Days	Hours	Average Speed
1	Lance Mackey	3/16 14:59:09	11	8	23	5.15
2	Hans Gatt	3/16 16:04:02	11	9	1	5.12
3	Jeff King	3/16 17:22:17	12	9	2	5.09
4	Ken Anderson	3/16 21:25:23	10	9	6	5.00
5	John Baker	3/16 22:07:54	9	9	7	4.98

March 20. Nome, Alaska. Only fifty-five of the seventy-two mushers and teams that began the 2010 race finish it. The last one crosses the finish line four days after Lance.

How many will be back to race again?

Lance Mackey, 2010 Iditarod Winner

Iditarod Records		
Musher	Year(s)	Records
Lance Mackey	2007-08-09-10	Most Consecutive Wins (4)
Robert Sorlie	2003	First Winner from Overseas
Martin Buser	2002	Fastest Winning Time
Doug Swingley	1995	First Winner from Outside Alaska
Libby Riddles	1985	First Woman to Win
Rick Swenson	1977-79-81-82-91	Most Times Won (5)
Mary Shields	1974	First Woman to Finish

The Inuit Keep Their Traditions Alive

"Listen, children. Listen to the beat of the drum."

Inuit elder Sara Olanna starts to play a flat, caribou-skin drum. Her husband, Joseph, begins to dance. He is wearing a wooden mask painted to look like a seal. And though he is in his eighties, he moves gracefully. He moves just like a swimming seal. As he dances, Sara sings. Her song thanks the seal for its meat and fur.

It's a special day for the Inuit children in Tanalipaq (tah-NAH-lee-pahk) Public School. They are getting their first lesson in drum dancing. It's one of the **oldest** Inuit traditions, about 5,000 years old. People like Sara and Joseph want to keep Inuit culture alive. And the children are eager to learn. To them, it is a part of their past they have heard about only in stories. But today, that past is coming alive.

Like any modern-day people, the Inuit of the Canadian Yukon shop in stores and supermarkets. They use trucks, cars, powerboats, and snowmobiles to get around. They live in wood and concrete houses. They watch television and listen to the radio. They read books and use computers. But they also remember their past. They honor their history through dancing, singing, storytelling, and art.

Less than 100 years ago, the Inuit were still living the same way they had lived for centuries. Proud of their traditional ways, they had also given themselves the name "Inuit," which means "the people."

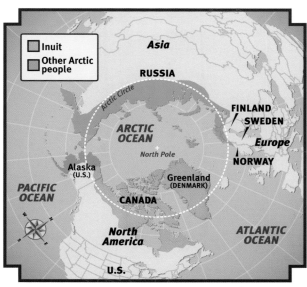

The Inuit people live in parts of Russia, Alaska, Canada, and Greenland.

Long ago, the Inuit had learned how to survive in the **harshest** climate. They tamed wild dogs and used them to pull sleds through the snow. In the spring and summer, they lived by inland rivers, where they fished for salmon. They hunted deer and caribou. They picked berries. In the autumn, they traveled to the coast. They used kayaks and large canoes to hunt whales, walruses, and seals. They dried the meat and fish so that they could have food through the long, dark, winter months.

The Inuit would live in different houses, depending on the seasons. In the spring and summer, they lived in tents made of wooden poles covered with caribou and deer skins. In the autumn and winter, they lived in underground homes by the sea. The homes were covered with mossy dirt, or sod. They slept on wooden boards covered with sealskins. They wore seal fur clothes and boots. And when they went hunting for seals and polar bears out on the ice, they built temporary houses called igloos. The igloos were made out of large blocks of ice and had rounded, dome-like roofs. Tunnel-like doorways were made by cutting openings in the thick ice.

13

Traditional Inuit drum dancers perform during a ceremony celebrating the creation of the Nunavut territory.

During the long winter from November to March, it was too dark and dangerous to hunt or fish. So the Inuit stayed inside. They spent the time sewing clothes and making hunting spears. They carved animals and made jewelry out of wood, metal, stone, and whalebone. They made painted wooden masks and animal-skin drums. And they told stories to the children. They told stories about how Earth was created. They told stories about past hunting adventures. The Inuit elders told the children tales about their ancestors. And the elders sang and danced.

For thousands of years, the Inuit handed down their stories, songs, and dances to their children. And their children did the same thing. But in the 1800s and 1900s, the Inuit began to lose their connection with their culture. Christian missionaries, European fur traders, and American gold miners began to settle in the Yukon. They brought their own ways of life. Often, the

Inuit ivory mask

Inuit were forced to give up their own language, traditions, and beliefs. Today, they still do some traditional hunting and fishing. But they also learned to hunt with guns, drive snowmobiles, and live in permanent houses.

Fortunately, a movement has grown among the Inuit to reclaim their past. Inuit public school children learn their native language, Inuktitut (ih-NOOK-tih-toot), along with English. They hold ceremonies that celebrate the seasons. And, like the children of Tanalipaq, they learn from their elders how to drum dance.

"Now, children, you dance, too," says Joseph Olanna. He holds out his arms. One by one, the children join him as Sara beats the drum and sings. Once again, the Inuit culture's **most glorious** past will live on in the Inuit people's future.

	Inuit Life of Centuries Ago	Inuit Life Today
Homes	tents, sod houses, igloos	wooden and concrete houses
Food	walrus, whales, seals, deer, caribou, salmon, berries	some traditional foods, mostly supermarket foods
Transportation	dog sleds, kayaks, canoes	cars, trucks, snowmobiles, powerboats
Clothing	animal furs and skins	some animal furs, mostly modern clothes
Hunting Tools	wooden spears, knives	guns
Language(s)	Inuktitut	Inuktitut, English
Entertainment	stories, dances, songs	books, TV, radio, computers, traditional stories, dances, songs

This chart compares how the Inuit lived long ago with modern-day Inuit life.

Analyze the Information in the Articles

- What are the articles about?
- How are the two articles similar?
- How are the two articles different?
- How does each article end?

Focus on Comprehension:
Identify Main Idea and Supporting Details

- On page 7, the author says "from its official beginning in 1973 and for years before, the Iditarod has been an annual contest of strength, skill, and endurance." What details support this stated main idea?
- Reread the section called "A Race That Honors Alaska's Past." What is the main idea of this section? Is the main idea stated or unstated?
- Pages 13 and 14 are about how the Inuit adapted to their location. What details support this unstated main idea?
- What is the main idea for the second-to-last paragraph of the article on the Inuit?

Analyze the Tools Writers Use:
Text and Graphic Features

- On page 8, the author includes a map and caption that describe the Iditarod routes. How does this graphic feature help readers understand the text?
- What text features does the author use in the Iditarod article? Remember, text features help readers locate information.
- What conclusion can you draw from the Inuit map on page 13?
- The author included a chart on page 15 that compares Inuit life long ago and today. What part of the text does this chart support?

Focus on Words: Superlatives

Make a chart like the one below. Locate each superlative in the articles. Identify which word the superlative is describing.

Page	Superlative	What word is the superlative describing?
7	most challenging	
7	most skillful	
7	most grueling	
12	oldest	
13	harshest	
15	most glorious	

The Yukon
GOLD RUSH: Surviving the Search for Wealth

Traveling through Canada's Yukon Territory is easy and enjoyable today. But it wasn't if you were a prospector hunting for gold in the late 1890s. If you were heading to Dawson City, a center for the Yukon Gold Rush, there was a good chance you might not make it. It was one of the **roughest**, **toughest** journeys anyone could make. You'd really have to want to do it. In fact, some people would call you crazy. They'd say you must have "gold fever."

In 1896, gold was discovered in the Yukon. More than 100,000 people hurried to claim a part of the treasure. Because so many prospectors arrived at the same time, the effect was like a herd of animals stampeding through. So the prospectors got the nickname "stampeders." What did it take to be a stampeder during the great Gold Rush? Do you think you could have handled the trip? And do you think you'd have been one of the lucky ones who got rich?

To begin the journey, you would have to make your way to one of the trails that led from America into Canada. Two of the **most popular** trails were the Chilkoot and White Pass trails. These roads were little more than rocky, muddy, icy paths. They took their toll on pack animals and wagons. And although you would have wanted to travel light, you would have had to bring a lot of supplies with you. Here is a partial list:

Food	Clothing	Supplies
400 lbs. of flour	2–3 suits of heavy underwear	4 heavy wool blankets, 4–6 towels
150 lbs. of bacon	2 heavy long shirts	1 tin of matches
25 lbs. of sugar	6 pairs of heavy wool socks	200 feet of rope
20–25 lbs. of dried potatoes	2 pairs of heavy rubber boots	10' x 12' canvas tent
15–20 lbs. of salt	1 heavy wool coat	5 yards of mosquito netting
75 lbs. of dried fruit	3 pairs of wool mittens, 1 pair of leather gloves	knife, axe, pick, shovel, saw, bucket, sharpening stone
100–125 lbs. of beans	1 stiff-brim cowboy hat	cooking pots and pans
10 lbs. coffee, 10 lbs. tea	1–2 pairs of overalls	1 sleeping bag

Prospectors needed to carry supplies weighing up to a ton per person.

In fact, you would have had to bring enough food, clothes, tents, and tools to last you a whole year! That was the law in Canada. No one could enter the country without carrying enough supplies. That was because many people starved to death before they even reached their destination.

You would have to have horses, oxen, and mules to pull your load. That was challenging enough. But the trip on the Yukon trails got even tougher the farther inland you traveled.

One half-mile (0.8-kilometer) section of the Chilkoot Trail was very steep. It was 1,000 feet (304.8 meters) high. To help prospectors get to the top, 1,500 steps were carved into the ice and snow. Imagine trying to climb that distance. Now imagine trying to haul a ton of supplies with you. Most stampeders left their animals behind. They carried loads of up to 60 pounds on their own backs. They went up and down the steps many times until all their supplies were at the top of the trail.

The White Pass Trail was no better. In fact, the weather conditions were much worse than on the Chilkoot Trail. A section of the White Pass Trail was so treacherous that more than 3,000 animals died. That section became known as the Dead Horse Trail.

If you survived the trails, you would arrive at the town of Whitehorse. From there you still had a 500-mile (804.7-kilometer) ride along the Yukon River. You, your supplies, and your animals would ride on a large paddle wheel steamboat. The boat's engine was powered by burning wood. So the boat would stop several times along the way to receive a load of logs cut from the nearby forests. Sometimes the steamboats caught on fire. Sometimes they hit ice and sank.

Farther along, your boat would arrive at Fort Selkirk, a welcome sight. Canadian troops protected the waterway from robbers and thieves. You could trade some of your goods for others. There you might find a doctor if you or your animals were sick.

Finally, you'd get to Dawson City. Now the toughest part of your work would begin. Thirty thousand people were crowded into the ramshackle town. They had already claimed most of the gold. You would be forced to try to find gold in an area where it was often buried more than 10 feet (3 meters) below the ground. As hard as it was to dig 10 feet down to see if there was gold, you couldn't even do that if you arrived in the winter. The ground was too frozen to dig!

If you survived the challenges and did manage to dig for gold, what were your chances of striking it big? Only a few stampeders became very rich. A few more earned about $5,000, enough to live on for a few years. Most found little or no gold. They quit and went back home. You might say they were "cured" of their gold fever.

Being a Gold Rush prospector was a hard, tough life. Do you think you could have been one of them? Would you have even wanted to?

The *Exxon Valdez* Oil Spill:
From Disaster to Recovery

Minutes after midnight on March 24, 1989, a 986-foot (300.5-meter) ship carrying crude oil hit a rocky reef in Alaska's Prince William Sound. Millions of gallons of oil started to gush from the bottom of the ship. The thick, black liquid spread quickly into the sea. No one could stop it. In six hours, 10.8 million gallons of oil—enough to fill nine school gymnasiums—flooded the icy waters. The accident of the tanker *Exxon Valdez* became one of the **largest** oil spills ever to take place in U.S. waters.

Officials of the government and the Exxon oil company reacted quickly. They sent hundreds of boats, airplanes, and helicopters to the area. Workers used machines to gather and suck up the oil. But they couldn't keep up with the pace at which the spill was spreading. Within a few days, the tides and currents spread the oil southwest. Eventually, 1,100 miles (1,770.3 kilometers) of Alaskan coastline were covered in black ooze.

ALASKA (U.S.)

Yukon River

CANADA

Valdez

Prince William Sound

Gulf of Alaska

This map shows how far and how quickly the *Exxon Valdez* oil spread.

Exxon Valdez ran aground here.

Valdez

Anchorage

Prince William Sound

CANADA

ALASKA

Area of map

KENAI PENINSULA

Cook Inlet

Homer

ALASKA

Day 4
March 27
37 miles

N
W E
S

Day 11
April 3
140 miles

ALASKA PENINSULA

KODIAK ISLAND

Gulf of Alaska

Day 19
April 14
250 miles

Day 56
May 18
470 miles

Day 40
May 2
350 miles

The accident caused enormous damage to the environment. The oil choked fish and sea mammals. It killed water plants. It coated the feathers of seabirds and proved to be fatal: The birds became extremely cold and were also unable to fly. The oil seeped into the beaches and stayed there. No one knows exactly how many living things died. At least twenty different kinds of creatures were affected. Among them, Alaskan officials estimated that approximately 250,000 seabirds, 2,800 sea otters, 300 harbor seals, 250 bald eagles, 22 killer whales, and billions of salmon and herring eggs were killed.

The author provides facts about how many animals were affected by the oil spill.

The author provides a primary source quote from a biologist involved in the cleanup efforts. The biologist's use of the superlative "most horrible" gives readers a firsthand account of the degree of the devastation.

The major concepts of the text are logically organized: The author first describes the oil spill and then details the response to it.

"It was the **most horrible** sight," said marine biologist Anne Pierce. "Thousands of us worked day and night for months. We washed the oil off ducks, seagulls, otters, and seals. We scooped up buckets and buckets of oily sand. We tried to make a difference."

From 1989 to 1992, biologists, fishermen, oil crews, and volunteers worked on the cleanup. More than 11,000 people, 1,400 boats, and 100 airplanes and helicopters were involved. According to the National Oceanic and Atmospheric Administration, it was "the largest oil spill cleanup ever mobilized."

The cleanup was also extremely expensive. Who paid for its cost? The U.S. government looked into the causes of the accident. They found that the *Exxon Valdez* wasn't steered or guided properly. The crew was overworked and overtired. So the government sued the Exxon oil company. Exxon paid more than $2 billion. The money covered the cost of cleaning the beaches and rescuing wildlife. But the oil spill had other effects. Many Alaskans' livelihoods were affected. Fishermen didn't catch as many fish. There was a shortage of food for seafood restaurants. Many tourists stopped coming to that part of Alaska. So hotels lost lots of business. Exxon paid another $1 billion to cover some of these damages as well.

The author provides facts on the cost of the cleanup.

Twenty-one years later, Prince William Sound looks pretty much like it did before the spill. Has the area completely recovered? That depends on whom you ask. Exxon claims that the cleanup is complete. But the U.S. government disagrees. According to the National Oceanic and Atmospheric Administration, a few beaches still have oil in them. Those beaches have fewer mussels and clams. Salmon fishermen say that the numbers of salmon are back to where they were before the spill. But herring fishermen report catching fewer fish than they did in 1989.

The author presents differing points of view from the U.S. government and Exxon, as well as from different fishermen.

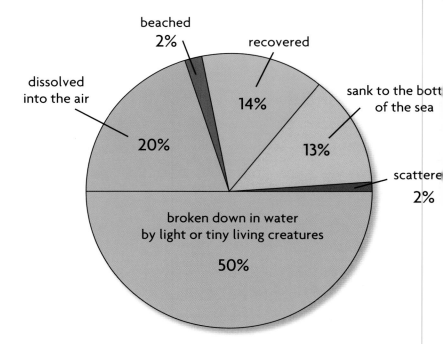

beached
2%

recovered

dissolved
into the air

sank to the bott
of the sea

14%

20%

13%

scattere
2%

broken down in water
by light or tiny living creatures

50%

**This pie chart shows what happened to
the oil that spilled from the *Exxon Valdez*.**

For Anne Pierce and other marine biologists, the work continues. They keep track of sea life in Prince William Sound. "It's taking a long time for the environment to recover," she says. "But I'm hopeful. More fish, birds, and animals are slowly making a comeback."

People have learned a lot from the *Exxon Valdez* accident. For one thing, Alaskan oil tankers now have thicker, stronger shells. The ships are guided more carefully through

Alaskan waters. Their movements are tracked by satellites. And scientists have developed better ways to clean up oil spills.

Pierce and her co-workers know how disastrous an oil spill can be. They hope that Prince William Sound will keep recovering. They hope that twenty-one years from now, the only place to find *Exxon Valdez* oil will be in history books.

The author's strong ending will keep readers thinking about the event and the environment.

Reread the Informational Texts

Analyze the Information in the Articles

- What are the articles about?
- How are the two articles similar?
- How are the two articles different?
- How does each article end?

Focus on Comprehension:
Identify Main Idea and Supporting Details

- Look at the article on the Yukon Gold Rush. What is the main idea for the last two paragraphs on page 20?
- The third and fourth paragraphs on page 21 are about the troubles in digging for gold. What details support this unstated main idea?
- Look at the article on the *Exxon Valdez*. What is the main idea in the paragraph on page 23 and the first paragraph on page 24? Is it a stated or unstated main idea?
- Reread the last paragraph on page 25 about the different viewpoints about the cleanup. What details support this unstated main idea?

Analyze the Tools Writers Use:
Text and Graphic Features

- Look at the article on the Yukon Gold Rush. What conclusion can you draw from the chart of supplies on page 19?
- The author included a map of the Yukon Territory on page 20. How does this graphic feature help readers understand the text?
- In the first paragraph of the *Exxon Valdez* article (page 22), the author uses a different font for the ship's name. How does that help readers?
- The map on page 23 shows how far and how quickly the *Exxon Valdez* oil spread. What part of the text does this map support?

Focus on Including Questions

Many authors include questions in their articles because they make readers stop and think about what they are reading. Identify places in the Yukon Gold Rush article where the author included questions. What do those questions make you think about?

Focus on Words: Superlatives

Make a chart like the one below. Locate each superlative in the articles. Identify which word the superlative is describing.

Page	Superlative	What word is the superlative describing?
18	roughest	
18	toughest	
19	most popular	
22	largest	
24	most horrible	

How does an author write an informational text?

**Reread "The *Exxon Valdez* Oil Spill: From Disaster to Recovery."
Think about what Jeanette Leardi did to write this informational text.
How did she keep a narrow focus? How did she help you understand
the text?**

1.

Decide on a Topic
Choose something you are interested in and want to know more about.
Good writers enjoy researching their topics.

2.

Narrow Your Focus
Jeanette Leardi knew she couldn't tell everything about the *Exxon
Valdez* oil spill, so she narrowed her focus to the cleanup efforts.

3.

Write a Question About Your Focus
Questions lead to answers, so turn your focus into a question.

4.

Research Your Focus
Become the expert by reading articles on the Internet, books, and
newspaper articles, and by interviewing people connected with your
topic. For example, Jeanette contacted the National Oceanic and
Atmospheric Administration for a lot of information about the disaster.
You want to show readers that you know what you are talking about.

5.

Organize Your Information
Before writing an informational article, make a chart or table like the
one on the next page that outlines the main points. For each main point,
identify supporting details. You don't have to write full sentences.
These are your notes. Remember, however, that there should be a
logical progression of ideas.

6.

Write Your Informational Text
As you write, develop each main point with your supporting details.
Remember that you want people to enjoy reading your article
as well as learn something new.

Topic: *Exxon Valdez* Oil Spill

Focus: Cleanup Effort

Question: What did it take to clean up all the oil that was spilled?

Main Point	Details
Introduction	*Exxon Valdez* oil spill occurred in 1989 in Alaska's Prince William Sound.
One of the worst oil spills in U.S. waters	Within six hours, 10.8 million gallons of oil were dumped into the water. Within a few days, 1,100 miles (1,770.3 kilometers of Alaskan coastline were covered in oil.
Officials reacted quickly	Hundreds of boats, airplanes, and helicopters were sent to the area, along with equipment to clean the spill.
More than twenty different kinds of living creatures were severely affected by the spill.	250,000 seabirds 2,800 sea otters 300 harbor seals 250 bald eagles 22 killer whales billions of salmon and herring eggs and more were estimated to be have been destroyed by the oil spill
The world's largest cleanup effort gets underway.	From 1989 to 1992, more than 11,000 people, 1,400 boats, and 100 airplanes and helicopters helped with the cleanup.
Cost of the cleanup	Exxon paid over $3 billion to the U.S. government to cover damages related to the spill.
Effects of the spill	Alaskan livelihoods were affected, including those of fishermen, food processing plant workers, restaurant and hotel workers, and all tourist industry professionals. A few beaches still have oil on them. Fish and seafood numbers have not rebounded completely.
Conclusion	More than two decades after the oil spill, the effects of it still remain, as do hopes that the area will someday be fully restored.

Glossary

harshest   (HAR-shest) most harsh; cruelest (page 13)

largest   (LAR-jest) biggest (page 22)

most challenging   (MOST CHA-len-jing) most difficult; hardest (page 7)

most glorious   (MOST GLOR-ee-us) most wonderful (page 15)

most grueling   (MOST GROO-ling) most exhausting (page 7)

most horrible   (MOST HOR-ih-bul) worst; most unpleasant (page 24)

most popular   (MOST PAH-pyuh-ler) most well liked (page 19)

most skillful   (MOST SKIL-ful) most proficient; expert (page 7)

oldest   (OLE-dest) most old (page 12)

roughest   (RUH-fest) most crude; most rugged (page 18)

toughest   (TUH-fest) most challenging (page 18)